D1326658

This book belongs to

10 9 8 7 6 5 4 3 2 1
© Copyright Catherine Mackenzie 2018
ISBN: 978-1-52710-117-3
Published by Christian Focus Publications, Geanies House, Fearn, Tain, Ross-shire, IV20 1TW, U.K.
Illustrations by Roger De Klerk; Cover design by Daniel van Straaten
Printed in China

All rights reserved. No part of this publication may be reproduced, stored in a retrieval system, or transmitted, in any form, by any means, electronic, mechanical, photocopying, recording or otherwise without the prior permission of the publisher or a licence permitting restricted copying. In the U.K. such licences are issued by the Copyright Licensing Agency, Saffron House, 6-10 Kirby Street, London, EC1 8TS. www.cla.co.uk

I SPY AT
CHRISTMAS

JESUS IS MORE IMPORTANT THAN CRACKERS AND TINSEL

CATHERINE MACKENZIE

ILLUSTRATED BY
ROGER DE KLERK

CF4•K

I spy a shiny **Christmas** tree with its decorations on.

So I think of Jesus the baby in the wooden manger. He made the trees. He made the animals that live in them and he made you. He's the Creator.

I spy the cold and frosty **Christmas** snow – brrr.

So I think of how God says that my sins are as red as scarlet but he can clean them. God can make my sins as white as snow.

I spy a fancy festive **Christmas** card.

So I think of how God wrote me a letter – the Bible. Why did he do that? He wants to tell me about my sin and his love.

I spy a **Christmas** present to open. It's very exciting. Hurray!
But it's even more exciting to think that God forgives me for my sins.
That's why Jesus was born, died and rose again.

I spy a **Christmas** cracker – snap! There are lovely surprises inside.

So I think of all the wonderful things that God has put inside the Bible for us: stories, songs, wonderful truths.

I spy someone singing a **Christmas** song – la la la!

So I think about how we should sing songs to God about how wonderful he is. He is the best!

I spy a shining Christmas star – sparkle sparkle. So I remember the star of Bethlehem and how God brought the wise men there.

I should listen to God's Word and trust in him – he will bring his children to heaven.

I spy some **Christmas** baking – yum. I know that delicious things are coming. So I remember that those who trust and love Jesus have the best times still to come. They are going to go to heaven.

I spy a yummy **Christmas** cake. It's decorated with frosting and a robin red-breast. So I thank God for food and for appetite.

God's Word is like tasty food.
Everything he says in the Bible is very good.

I spy an empty **Christmas** stocking. It is going to be filled up with good things.

So I remember that God wants me to be filled with love for him.

I spy **Christmas** wrapping paper. I'm going to send a parcel to someone I love.

So I will remember to send my love to God by turning away from the bad things I do and loving him instead.

I spy the sparkly **Christmas** lights. They brighten up all the dark spaces. God's Word is like a light – the very best and brightest light.

God shows me what is true and what is false.

I spy a **Christmas** snowman with a scarf and hat.
So I remember that snowmen do not last forever.
The sun comes out and they melt away.
But God's Word lasts for ever.

I spy a pretty **Christmas** wreath with holly and ivy. It's very pretty. I will hang it up for all to see.

By loving and obeying Jesus my life is beautiful. Others will see how lovely Jesus is when I love and obey him.

I spy **Christmas** cards waiting to be posted. It's lovely to get good news. So I remember that the best news ever is that God sent his Son Jesus to save us from sin.

I spy a **Christmas** concert. I like to watch and listen.

So I remember that God hears and watches me all the time.

I spy a **Christmas** ribbon and bow. I could stick it on a present or tie it on the tree.

So I remember that though a ribbon ties things together, I don't need a ribbon to tie me to God. God will never leave me.

I spy a **Christmas** candy cane. It's sweet. I remember that there are two colours, white and red. Red reminds me of how Jesus died to save sinners. White reminds me of how he washes away my sin.

I spy a **Christmas** candle. It lights up the dark. So I remember that I can be a bright light for Jesus. I can tell others that Jesus is full of forgiveness, love and life. He is the light of the world.

I spy Santa in his red suit – ho ho ho.
Presents are on the way at **Christmas**.

So I remember that God's gifts are better than Santa's. Jesus, his Son, is the best gift, the perfect gift. Jesus is real and his gifts last forever.

I spy an advent calendar. I'll count the days until the 25th of December. So I remember that **Christmas** day is just one day of fun.

Those who trust in Jesus have heaven to look forward to – good times with Jesus that will never end.

I spy a **Christmas** hat which looks like a crown. So I remember that God is King of everything and everyone. He is in charge.

I spy a **Christmas** party. It's lots of fun. Everyone is together. So I remember that one day all the people who love God will be together and will sing and shout joyfully to God.

I spy a **Christmas** bell. I hear it ring out – ding dong. So I remember that everyone needs to hear about Jesus.
The clock strikes midnight. Now it's **Christmas**. I thank God for the gift of his Son, Jesus. **Christmas** is only once a year – but God listens and loves every day of the year.

CHRISTIAN FOCUS PUBLICATIONS

Christian Focus Publications publishes books for adults and children under its four main imprints: Christian Focus, CF4K, Mentor and Christian Heritage. Our books reflect our conviction that God's Word is reliable and Jesus is the way to know him, and live for ever with him. Our children's list includes a Sunday School curriculum that covers pre-school to early teens, and puzzle and activity books. We also publish personal and family devotional titles, biographies and inspirational stories that children will love. If you are looking for quality Bible teaching for children, then we have an excellent range of Bible stories and age-specific theological books. From pre-school board books to teenage apologetics, we have it covered!

Christian Focus Publications Ltd, Geanies House, Fearn, Ross-shire, IV20 1TW, Scotland, U.K.

www.christianfocus.com